KNOW HOW KNOW WHY

FLIGHT

Written by Colin Dibben

Illustrations by Mike Thomas

www.rourkepublishing.com

Library of Congress Cataloging-in-Publication Data

Dibben, Colin -
    Flight / Colin Dibben.
        p. cm. -- (Know How, Know Why)
    Includes Bibliographical references and index
    ISBN 1-60044-259-5 (hardcover)
    ISBN 978-1-60044-347-3 (paperback)

Printed in the USA

CG/CG

Rourke Publishing

www.rourkepublishing.com – sales@rourkepublishing.com
Post Office Box 3328, Vero Beach, FL 32964

THE PIONEERS

People have been trying to fly like birds for hundreds of years. However, until 1903 no one knew how to power or control a flying machine.

Cables were used to move the wings.

Who were the Wright brothers

Wilbur and Orville Wright were two Americans who really wanted to fly! The brothers built gliders and kites for years—and then, on December 17 1903, they became the first people to fly a powered aircraft. Their airplane was called *The Flyer* and it flew for twelve seconds and 120 feet (36.5 m) at Kitty Hawk in North Carolina.

Wilbur and Orville Wright.

The Flyer remained airborne for twelve seconds!

What did they do next

Wilbur and Orville set up the world's first test flight facilities and perfected a series of aircraft designs. Their next step was to develop a military aircraft that they could sell in both Europe and America. By 1909, they were famous around the world as successful inventors who had changed history forever.

Who were the other pioneers

The Wright brothers won the race to build a powered aircraft that could fly. Their main rival was Samuel Langley, a professor who built a flying machine called an aerodrome. Aerodromes used steam engines and were much too heavy to fly. Of course, by 1903, people had been flying in gliders and balloons for some years.

An aerodrome was powered by a 52 hp engine.

How did *The Flyer* fly ?

The Flyer flew because Wilbur and Orville discovered how to make an aircraft roll like a bird does in flight. They used cables to move the wings and the wings steered the aircraft. The brothers used two propellers to produce thrust to make the aircraft go forward and a petrol engine to power their machine.

Propellers rotated to produce thrust to move the aircaft forward.

A petrol engine was used to power the aircraft.

Who built the first aircraft ?

The ancient Chinese were the first people to try to fly, inspired by their love of kites. They used kites in religious ceremonies and to test the weather—as well as for fun. The Renaissance artist Leonardo da Vinci designed a flying machine called an ornithopter that used levers and pulleys to give more power to the pilot's arms and legs.

An ornithopter mimicked a bird's winged flight.

EARLY WAYS TO FLY

Early aircraft were difficult to get off the ground and keep in the air. Designers looked at kites and gliders to find out how to improve their airplanes.

Why were kites important in the early days of flight

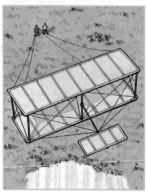

An early "Wright kite."

The Wright brothers built and flew a large kite to test their twisty or "wing-warping" flight-control system. The kite showed them that cables could be used to control wings. After the brothers had finished, they gave the kite away to local children. Replicas of the "Wright kite" can be found in museums all over the world.

How do gliders work ?

Gliders are airplanes without engines. They must be launched, but take off is easy because their long, narrow wings generate a lot of lift. Lift is the force that lifts an aircraft off the ground. Once in the air, gliders travel on "thermals," columns of air rising off Earth. To land, the pilot increases the air resistance or "drag" with brakes on the wings.

The Red Baron's Fokker Triplane.

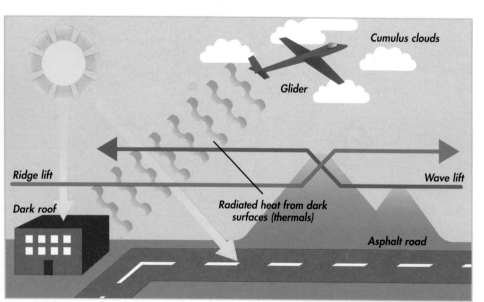

Cumulus clouds

Glider

Ridge lift

Wave lift

Dark roof

Radiated heat from dark surfaces (thermals)

Asphalt road

Gliders travel on columns of air called thermals.

FACT BYTES

During re-entry to Earth's atmosphere, the Space Shuttle acts just like a glider, floating all the way down to the runway at Cape Canaveral.

When was the first glider flight ?

In 1849, a servant boy became the first person in history to fly when British designer, George Cayley, strapped him into a glider. Cayley later flew a manned triplane glider and this sort of glider became very popular. Forty years later, brave hang glider Otto Lilienthal used biplane gliders for many of his record-breaking 2,500 flights.

Manned triplane gliders were once very popular.

Why do some planes have extra wings ?

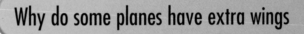

Airplanes with two or three wings on top of each other (know as bi and triplanes) were made famous by the first fighter pilots. At low speeds, these stacked wings increase the lift of an airplane. They also improve the aircraft's ability to change direction or maneuver. Biplanes were popular until the 1930s, when speeds increased because of better engines.

Who was the Red Baron ?

The German pilot Baron von Richthofen is probably the most famous fighter ace of all time. He was called the Red Baron because he painted his Fokker triplane red. During World War One, he shot down 80 French and English planes before being shot and killed in 1918 at the age of 25.

At low speeds stacked wings help increase lift.

The Red Baron.

FACT BYTES

Otto Lilienthal inspired all aviators when he said:

"To invent an airplane is nothing. To build one is something. But to fly is everything."

CHANNEL HOPPERS

The English Channel may be only 21 miles (33.8 km) across, but it remains one of the great challenges for record-breakers in aircraft of all sorts.

Why is crossing the Channel such a challenge

Flying across the Channel was a tradition started by balloonists. Early airplanes often broke down after just twenty minutes' flight. Pilots hated crossing water because they knew that if they crashed in the sea they would probably die. Pilots saw the English Channel as wide enough to be dangerous without being impossible.

Crossing the Channel was difficult but not impossible.

Channel hopping was started by balloonists.

Who was the first to fly across the Channel

Louis Bleriot.

On July 25 1909, French aviator Louis Blériot landed a small airplane near Dover Castle, UK. On the way over from France, Blériot got lost in fog (he forgot to pack a compass!) but the fog's moisture kept his engine from overheating. He made the journey in 37 minutes and won £1000, which was the prize the London *Daily Mail* newspaper gave to the first person to fly across the Channel.

Fog kept Blériot's engine from over-heating.

Why was Blériot's crossing important

This 37-minute flight was the second great feat of aviation history. It made people realize that countries—even islands like Britain—could be attacked from the air. The famous British prime minister, Lloyd George, drew attention to this danger and called for an "air force" to help defend Britain, saying that "flying machines are no longer toys and dreams, they are established fact."

Lloyd George.

Who was the first woman to cross the Channel

Harriet Quimby was the first American woman to learn to fly and is one of the great personalities in early aviation. She always wore a plum-colored satin suit and a fur scarf when flying. On April 16 1912 she flew over the Channel from Dover to Calais. Sadly, she died in an airplane accident ten weeks later.

Harriet Quimby.

Harriet Quimby was the first American woman to fly.

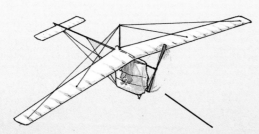

The Gossamer Albatross was a sort of "flying bicycle."

What other aircraft have crossed

In 1977, the *Gossamer Albatross*, a sort of flying bicycle, became the first aircraft to be pedaled across the Channel! The designer of the *Albatross*, Paul MacCready, went on to build the first aircraft driven by solar power. In 1979, the *Solar Challenger* flew 180 miles (290 km) over the Channel.

Gossamer Albatross.

Felix Baumgartner skydived across the Channel in 2003.

What is the newest record

To celebrate 100 years of aviation, Felix Baumgartner skydived across the Channel on the July 31 2003. Felix was only wearing a special suit with a wing attached to it. He reached speeds of 217 mph (349 kph). Afterwards, Felix said: "Blériot did it with a plane, I did it with a little wing."

AROUND THE WORLD

Just twenty years after the Wright brothers' first flight, biplanes flew around the world. Records have been made and broken ever since in this ultimate aviation challenge.

When did the first flight take place

On April 6 1924, four US Army Air Corps biplanes took off from Seattle, America. They landed there again 175 days later, after a journey of 26,000 miles (41,834 km). The flight took so long because the crews were just trying to fly around the world—they didn't care how long it took. In fact, the men had holidays all over the world!

A US Army Air Corps Biplane.

US Army pilots flew around the world in 1924.

FACT BYTES

The Space Shuttle circumnavigates Earth in just 90 minutes because it is easier to fly above Earth's atmosphere.

Who was the first pilot to fly solo around the world **?**

After losing an eye in an accident, Wiley Post learned to fly in just 100 minutes. Then he bought himself a plane called *Winnie Mae* and flew solo around the world in 7 days, 18 hours and 49 minutes in 1933. Wiley did all the flying and navigating—he even made a machine in the cockpit to wake him up if he fell asleep!

Mae Wells, Post's key help on the ground, stands beside the Winnie Mae.

FACT BYTES

The Sun rose and set three times during Concorde's record-breaking round-the-world flight in August 1995. It flew faster than Earth rotates— 1 mile (1.6 km) every 2.5 seconds.

When were the fastest flights **?**

In 1949, the US Air Force notched up the first non-stop round-the-world tour in just 94 hours. In 1997, a Malaysian Airlines Boeing 777 took 42 hours, but supersonic Concorde holds the current record at 31 hours 27 minutes and 49 seconds in 1995.

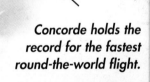

Concorde holds the record for the fastest round-the-world flight.

Why do long distance flights take so long **?**

Early planes were slow and pilots had to stop to refuel. The subsonic and supersonic jets that set the time records can either refuel in mid air (from other aircraft), or carry lots of fuel themselves. No commercial airplane can beat Concorde's speed record, but a stealth military aircraft can because it travels much, much faster!

Stealth military aircraft.

What other sorts of aircraft have made the journey **?**

In 1986, a very light, hi-tech aircraft called *Voyager* flew around the world in nine days without stopping or refueling. Even more impressive is the story of Colin Bodrill, who successfully flew a microlight around the world in 2000!

Voyager flew 24,986 miles (40,211 km) in nine days.

AROUND THE WORLD

THE JET ENGINE

The jet engine caused a revolution in modern life changing everything from the way we go on vacation to the way we go to war.

What is a jet engine ?

A jet engine throws out a powerful jet of air that is used for "thrust," the force that pushes an aircraft forward. Air is drawn into a jet engine, "pressurized" (which means put under pressure), mixed with fuel and then burnt. The burning mixture roars out of the engine at over 1,243 mph (2,000 km/h), providing the aircraft with enormous thrust.

One of four jet engines found on this military plane.

Who built the first one ?

In ancient Greece, Hero of Alexander made a very simple jet engine called an aeolipile, which used jets of steam to create movement. In the 1930s, the Germans and the British raced each other to produce a jet engine. British inventor Frank Whittle made the first jet engine in 1937, but the Germans were able to fly the first jet airplane.

Steam from the cauldron traveled along hollow tubes to turn the hollow sphere called "the aeolipile."

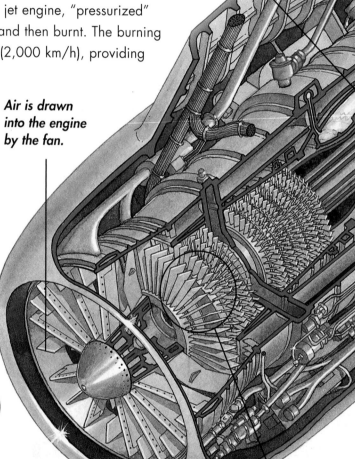

The air is mixed with fuel and burnt.

Air is drawn into the engine by the fan.

Air is pressurized by turbines.

FACT BYTES

The success of the jet engine is based around Isaac Newton's Third Law of Motion, which states that "every action has an equal and opposite reaction." Simply—the backward force of a jet engine moves the plane forwards.

A single Boeing 777 jumbo jet engine produces more thrust than the eight engines of an enormous B-52 bomber.

Boeing 737s have carried 4.3 billion passengers, which is equal to half the world's population.

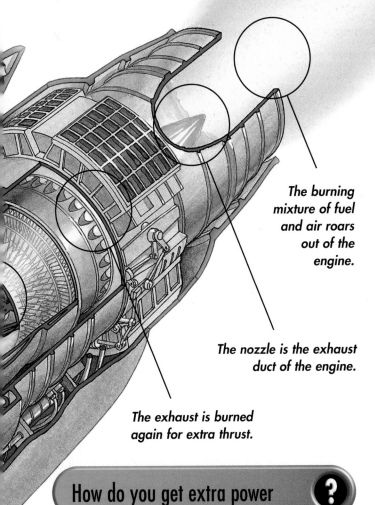

The burning mixture of fuel and air roars out of the engine.

The nozzle is the exhaust duct of the engine.

The exhaust is burned again for extra thrust.

Why is the jet important

Because the thrust of a jet engine is so powerful, aircraft can be made bigger and fly faster and further. Jet engines have made traveling abroad possible for millions of people, in planes carrying 500 people, or more. Jet engines also enable warplanes to fly across the world a lot faster, and are very reliable. Some also have computers which radio ahead if there are engine problems.

A passenger jet.

How do you get extra power

Gases that roar from a jet engine are called the jet's exhaust. As they rush out, these gases turn turbines that pressurize the air entering the front of the engine. The gases are burned again, to provide extra thrust. Fighter planes use these "after-burners" in combat and for high-speed take offs.

How big are jumbo jets

Some of the biggest jets in the world are passenger-carrying aircraft known as jumbo jets. The biggest is the Boeing 747, which carries 600 people and travels at 565 mph (910 km/h). The smaller 777 broke the subsonic round-the-world speed record by flying at 553 mph (889 km/h). A new plane, the Airbus A380, will carry 800 people and travel at 595 mph (955 km/h).

Figher jets use "after-burners."

The Airbus A380.

THE JET ENGINE

TAKE OFF!

Discover all you need to know about the complicated business of getting aircraft off the ground—and then keeping them in the air!

What happens at take off

There are four forces involved in flight: lift, weight, thrust, and drag. Lift keeps an aircraft flying and is created by the wings moving through the air. The aircraft's weight prevents it leaving the ground. Thrust propels the aircraft through the air and is produced by the engine. Drag is the air that flows against the aircraft, stopping it from moving forward.

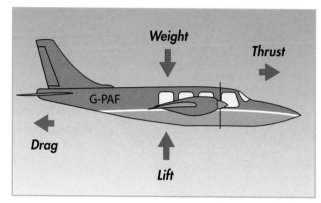

Flight involves four forces.

How do aircraft get into the air

Aircraft use the lift created by their wings to counteract their weight. When air flows over wings, the shape of the wing sucks the wing upwards, lifting the aircraft. The wing must be moving, so an aircraft needs the thrust provided by the engines. Finally, an aircraft has to push air out of its way, and thrust helps here too.

How do aircraft stay in the air

Once in the air, an aircraft must keep producing enough lift to counteract air drag and its own weight. The shape of the wing helps lift the airplane, but if the airplane loses thrust, air will not travel fast enough past the wing. Then the wing will stop producing lift and the aircraft stalls.

When air flows over the wings, the plane lifts.

Who is the air traffic controller

Airplanes fly in and out of very busy airports. Air traffic controllers are the people who control this flow of aircraft. They sit in a tower with lots of windows to one side of the runway. From there, they check that there is a safe distance between aircraft and order all their movements. This job is difficult—it has been described as playing chess in 3-D.

An air traffic control tower.

How are aircraft controlled ❓

Most modern aircraft are controlled by computers, but pilots still need cockpit controls. Pilots use foot pedals to turn the rudder. The rudder turns the plane left or right. Pilots move a control stick from side to side to move the ailerons (flaps attached to the wings) which provide better control when turning. Pilots move the stick backwards or forwards to move the elevators, which pitch the plane up or down.

The cockpit controls contain foot pedals (center) to turn the rudder.

The shape of the wings help lift the aircraft.

If an airplane loses thrust, it can stall.

What happens when an aircraft stalls ❓

When an aircraft stalls, it literally falls out of the sky! Jet fighters stall all the time because they fly at very steep angles, and this affects the flow of air over the wings. It's easy to recover from a stall—all the pilot has to do is point the "nose" or front of the aircraft downwards to increase speed, or turn the throttle for more thrust.

FACT BYTES

An airliner will stall if it goes much slower than 150 mph (240 km/h).

Designers give aircraft streamlined shapes so that they are less affected by drag.

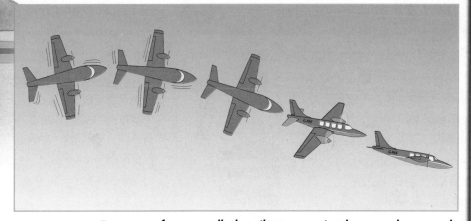

To recover from a stall, the pilot must point the nose downwards and increase speed.

TAKE OFF!

TOUCHDOWN!

Landing an aircraft is even more dangerous and exciting than take off—the pilot needs a keen eye, nerves of steel, and a steady hand.

How does a pilot land a jumbo jet ?

Five miles (8 km) from the airport, the pilot descends to 2,000 feet (610 m) and lowers the speed of the airplane to 200 mph (320 kph). At 3 miles (4.8 km) from the airport, the pilot lines the nose of the aircraft up with the runway and drops the landing gear. The pilot keeps the pitch of the aircraft at three degrees and brakes when the landing gear touches the ground.

The pilot descends and lowers the speed.

The landing gear is dropped.

The pilot brakes when the plane touches the ground.

What is the brace position ?

If the pilot needs to make an emergency landing, he or she will tell the passengers to adopt a "brace position" for their safety. This involves putting your head between your knees and clasping your shins with your hands—until the plane comes to a complete stop.

The brace position.

What part does landing gear play ?

The wheels that hang below the airplane are called landing gear. During flight, the landing gear is kept inside the plane so that it doesn't create drag and slow the airplane down. During take off and landing and while the airplane is on the ground, the landing gear is lowered.

Landing gear.

How does a pilot land safely ❓

Pilots must concentrate on three things—the altitude, airspeed and angle of approach of their aircraft. These are all controlled by the throttle (which allows the pilot to increase or decrease the power of the engines) and the pitch of the plane, which the pilot can change using the elevators. The pilot must be very careful not to stall the plane at low altitudes.

The throttle allows pilots to increase or decrease power.

FACT BYTES

Pilots are trained to glide a plane that has no working engines and no fuel back to the ground.

Just before landing a jumbo jet is still traveling at a rate of 175 mph (281 km/h).

Why do landings go wrong ❓

Pilots are very well trained and landings hardly ever go wrong. But they sometimes do, for a variety of reasons. If an airplane lands too fast it over-runs the runway. If it is traveling too slow on approaching the runway, it stalls and crashes. In fact, most landings go wrong because the airplane is going too fast. Bad approaches can also be caused by bad weather conditions such as ice, air turbulence or severe winds.

Why not just switch off the engine ❓

Pilots take pride in landing airplanes on the first third of the airport runway, and they do this simply by controlling the aircraft's thrust, lift and drag. If you switch off the engine and glide down it is more difficult to judge whether the aircraft will slow down enough by the time it lands.

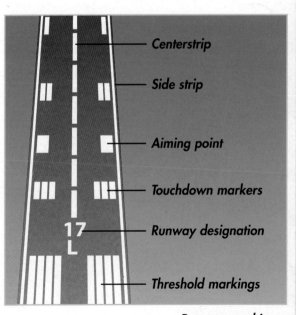

— Centerstrip

— Side strip

— Aiming point

— Touchdown markers

— Runway designation

— Threshold markings

Runway markings.

MATERIAL MAGIC

The heavier an aircraft, the more fuel it burns. So, ever since the first wooden airplanes, aviation engineers have searched for lighter, stronger materials.

What were early aircraft made from ?

The Wright brothers' *Flyer* was made out of a light fabric attached to a wooden frame. Early aircraft were made from wood and canvas because these materials were light and available. Most of the 170,000 airplanes built during World War One had fabric stretched over wooden frames, which helped strengthen them. Wooden aircraft could be quite sophisticated— light woods were often molded to streamline aircraft.

Wood and canvas were lightweight and easily available.

What was the biggest wooden aircraft ?

During World War Two, millionaire Howard Hughes designed an enormous cargo airplane. It was made entirely from wood in order to help save metal for the war effort. The 3000,000 lb (135,000 kg) aircraft, nicknamed the "Spruce Goose," had a wingspan of 318 feet (97 m)! It flew only once, in 1947, with Hughes at the controls himself.

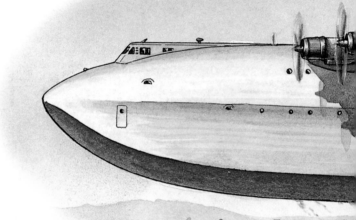

When was the first metal aircraft made ?

Hugo Junkers, a German designer, built an all-metal aircraft just before World War One, but the first all-metal commercial airplane, the Pullman, arrived in 1924. Aluminum is the best metal for airplanes. Aluminum is stronger than wood and allows planes to go faster. But aluminum is expensive, so scientists developed alloys, which are cheaper, stronger mixtures of metals and non-metals.

A 1920's Junkers JL-6, an early metal plane.

Hugo Junkers.

What are airplanes made of today **?**

Composites are combinations of materials that hold together and reinforce each other. Fiberglass is the most common composite, graphite is another. Fiberglass was first used in the Boeing 707 passenger jet of the 1950s. Composites are incredibly light and strong, but very expensive to make and mend. So, airliners are still made from aluminum alloys, while military aircraft use composite materials.

Military aircraft are made from composite materials.

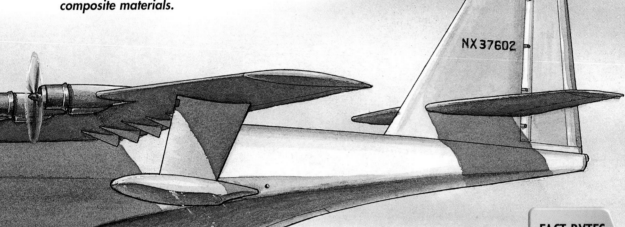

The "Spruce Goose" was a huge wooden cargo plane.

FACT BYTES

The deHavilland Mosquito was made almost entirely out of wood. It could fly faster and higher than other World War Two warplanes.

How was the Boeing 777 made **?**

The Boeing 777 is the biggest twin-engine aircraft ever. It cost $4 billion to make and was designed completely on computers (2,200 of them!). About ten percent of the Boeing 777 is made up of composite materials like graphite and fiberglass as well as a super-strong substance called hybrid.

The Boeing 777 was designed on computers.

MATERIAL MAGIC

FIGHTER PLANES

Fighters were specially designed to attack and destroy other aircraft. For this sort of work, agility and "maneuverability' are just as important as speed!

When did airplanes first attack each other ?

"Dog-fights" took place during World War One.

Early airplanes were used by armies to spy on enemy troops. When airplanes from warring sides met in the air, trouble was inevitable. The first aerial combat took place in November 1913, during the Mexican Civil War, when pilots fired pistols at each other. By 1915, specially armed fighting scouts were engaged in dog-fights (close-quarter combat) over the trenches of Northern France.

What sort of weapons do fighters have ?

The World War One fighting scouts had machine-guns fixed to the airplane in front of the pilot. During World War Two, powerful machine guns or cannon that fired explosive ammunition were placed in wings. Since 1958, fighters have been armed with guided air-to-air missiles. These deliver an explosive warhead and are either guided by radar or home-in on a heat source like an engine exhaust. A fighter armed with missiles can fire on enemy aircraft 100 miles away. Powerful lazer weapons for fighters are being developed, which will destroy hostile aircraft at the speed of light!

FACT BYTES

The machine guns on World War One fighters could fire between the spinning propeller blades.

An estimated 22,579 Supermarine Spitfires served in all spheres of World War Two and afterwards.

In World War One, pilots were armed with machine guns.

What were the first jet fighters ?

Propeller-driven fighters started to look like dinosaurs on July 12 1944—the day the British Gloster Meteor became the world's first jet fighter. The German Messerschmitt Me 262 zoomed into combat just two weeks later. The Me 262 could reach a speed of 540 mph (864 km/h). Unfortunately, it rattled a lot and became unstable at high speed. Although it was fast, the Me 262 was not as agile as some of its opponents.

The Me 262 was fast and deadly but it rattled dangerously.

In 1944, the Gloster Meteor became the world's first jet fighter.

FACT BYTES

The MiG-29 "Fulchrum" was designed to destroy air targets from 37-124 miles (60-200 km) in all weather conditions and altitudes!

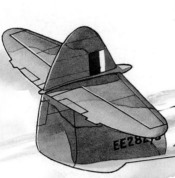

The Russian MiG-15 flew 8 miles (13 km) high during the Korean War.

Where can you see the famous fighters ?

Every summer, fighter planes take part in air shows —unarmed of course! You can see jet fighters like the Eurofighter and the Harrier. You can also see older fighters like Spitfires and Hurricanes that have been restored. Large museums will often have a selection of these aircraft too.

Air shows are a good place to see restored fighters.

BOMBERS

Bombers attack targets on the ground. They must travel high and fast to evade the fighter aircraft that try to shoot them out of the sky.

When were the first bombers flown

The Italians were the first to use bombers, against the Turkish in Libya in 1912. During World War One, German Zeppelins bombed Paris and London. In reply, the British sent their largest airplane, the Handley Page 0/100, to bomb factories in Germany. This was the first "strategic bombing," which means the bombing of factories and cities rather than enemy soldiers.

Zeppelins were used to bomb Paris and London.

What is a dive bomber

A dive bomber dives down on its targets, making a screaming noise as it rushes through the air. This is terrifying for people on the ground and dangerous for the pilot too, because the dive bomber is flying very low and can easily be attacked by fighters. The Japanese Kamikaze were bomber pilots who went on suicide missions against American ships.

"Strategic bombing" targeted factories.

A Japanese dive bomber.

Which is the most successful bomber

The B-52 Stratofortress was designed during World War Two to bomb Germany from America. The wings of the B-52 are extremely long and thin, which helps the plane fly very high. First flown in 1952, the B-52 carries 70,000 lb (32,400 kg) of bombs. The plane is best known for its bombing missions during the Vietnam War but was recently used in Iraq and Afghanistan.

The World War Two B-52 is still in use today.

What is a Lancaster ?

The Avro Lancaster is the most famous British bomber. It is often called the "workhorse" of the bombing campaign against Nazi-occupied Europe. This is because Lancasters flew an amazing 156,000 missions during World War Two. The Lancaster had powerful Rolls-Royce engines and a very accurate target finder.

FACT BYTES

On 15th September, 1944, Lancasters sank the German battleship *Tirpitz* with three enormous 12,000 lb (5,400 kg) Tallboy bombs.

Lancasters were used during the famous Dambuster mission.

A Tornado

A F1-11

A Mosquito

What are "fighter-bombers" ?

Some bombers are smaller, faster and more agile than strategic bombers like the Lancaster and the B-52. They can carry out attacks on other aircraft and on targets on the ground. These aircraft are called "fighter-bombers." Famous examples are the Mosquito, the F1-11 and the Tornado.

PLANES AT WAR

Air combat is central to winning battles and wars on the ground. Aircraft have changed warfare forever and played an important role in modern history.

Why are warplanes important ❓

Bombers and fighters are essential for winning wars. Hitler's plan to invade England failed because his air force lost the Battle of Britain and World War Two ended because planes dropped two atomic bombs on Japan. In both Gulf Wars, strategic bombing and smart bombs dropped by multi-role aircraft devastated the Iraqi army, making it safer for Allied ground troops to fight.

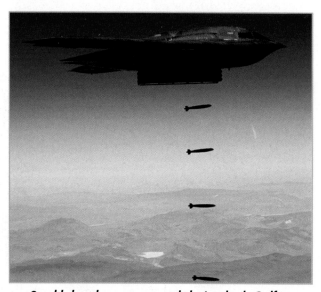

Stealth bombers were used during both Gulf wars.

When was the Battle of Britain ❓

Between July and October 1940, the German Air Force flew 1300 bombers and 1200 fighters against 750 Royal Air Force fighters. Casualties were horrific on both sides, but the RAF's Supermarine Spitfires and Hawker Hurricanes won a great victory. Britain's radar and supply of new fighters helped win the battle, as did Germany's lack of strategic bombers.

The great Supermarine Spitfire.

The Battle of Britain took place in 1940.

Why is speed not enough ?

A warplane must be fast, but also well-armed, able to fly high and maneuver well. Some modern jet fighters have wings that can move to a "swept" position nearer the "fuselage" or body of the plane. The normal position gets the aircraft off the ground, while the swept position makes it move and turn much faster in the air.

"Swept-back" wings help planes to move faster.

A deadly Messerschmitt Bf 109.

FACT BYTES

The Hawker Harrier doesn't need a runway—it takes off vertically with the help of small, powerful jets that can be pointed straight down.

The Supermarine Spitfire had special elliptical wings that made it easy to maneuver fast, which is essential in dogfights.

Famous planes fought over Southern England.

What is warplane camouflage ?

Aircraft attacking targets on the ground are painted green and brown, the colors of vegetation, so that they blend into their environment. Strategic bombers, interceptors, and aircraft intended for dogfighting are painted light blue or gray. This makes it harder for an enemy plane to see them in the sky. Hiding military activity in this way is called "camouflage."

How warplanes changed ?

The makers of fighters and bombers compete against each other. The first bombers created a need for interceptor fighters that could shoot them down. So then strategic bombers were designed to fly much higher, while attack bombers were armed better and flew nearer the ground. Today, fighters and bombers still go faster and higher in order to destroy each other!

Aircraft are camouflaged using blue or gray paint.

LIGHTER THAN AIR

What is the connection between balloons you play with and the enormous airships that are used to fly across the ocean?

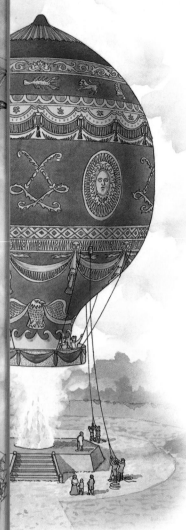

Fire was used to create "hot air."

Who built the first balloon

The Montgolfier brothers made a balloon out of paper and linen and attached a basket to it. On September 17 1783, the brothers built a fire in the basket, popped in a sheep, a duck and a chicken—and watched as the balloon soared to 1,700 feet (518 m). Two months later, the first manned, lighter-than-air flight ascended to 3,000 feet (914 m) above Paris.

The Montgolfier brothers.

How does a balloon work

The Montgolfiers' balloon rose because of the heat generated by the fire. Hot air rises because it is less "dense" or heavy than cold air. The hot air inside a balloon is hotter than the air outside, so the air rises, taking the balloon "shell" with it. Balloon flight is called "lighter-than-air" flight because the air inside the balloon really is lighter than normal air.

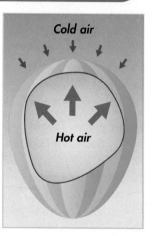

Cold air

Hot air

Hot air inside the balloon is lighter than the colder air outside.

FACT BYTES

The Montgolfier brothers were inspired to build a balloon when they saw a shirt that had been left to dry over a fire.

113,746 feet = US Navy officers Ross and Prather, 1961.

51,744 feet = Auguste Piccard's record, 1931.

1000 feet = Most balloon flights will rise to here.

500 feet = Balloon journeys start to become fun!

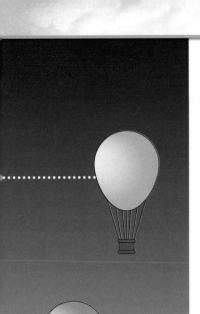

How far can a balloon travel

Most flights using balloons occur between 500-1,000 feet (152-304 m). Auguste Piccard became the first human to reach the stratosphere when he rose to 51,744 feet (15,780 m) in a balloon on May 27 1931. The current altitude record is 113,746 feet (34,668 m). The *Breitling Orbiter 3* made the first non-stop trip around the world by balloon in 1999.

Auguste Piccard.

What is a Zeppelin

Balloons are very difficult to steer. You can make a balloon "dirigible" (which simply means "controllable") by squashing it and adding an engine. The squashed shape helps reduce drag. Ferdinand von Zeppelin made "rigid dirigibles" that had taut fabric shells. By the 1930s, Zeppelins were taking passengers across the Atlantic in under three days.

A Zeppelin.

Why did the *Hindenburg* explode

The *Hindenburg* was the largest and most famous zeppelin. It exploded on May 6 1937, upon landing in America. The giant hydrogen bags that kept the airship afloat were blamed. It now seems likely that the fabric shell ignited. Because of this terrible disaster, airships are no longer used for public transport.

The **Hindenburg** *disaster led to the demise of airships.*

LIGHTER THAN AIR

SAFETY FIRST

Flying is an incredibly safe way to travel. When something does go wrong, everyone tries to stop it from happening again.

How safe is flying ?

Flying is the safest form of transport. You are 50 times safer in a commercial jet than in a car. This is because aircraft makers are constantly improving aircraft safety. Airliners undergo mechanical checks every 100 hours, and pilots have continuous training and medical checks. Thirty years ago, only one person died out of every two million people who traveled by airplane. Now the risk is one in ten million!

Why are emergency exits important ?

The passengers board an airliner through large doors at the front or the back of the airplane. Along the fuselage or body of the plane, there are extra exits that passengers can use if an emergency occurs. It is important for everyone on board to know where their nearest emergency exit is—so that if something does go wrong they can escape as quickly as possible.

Why should you listen to the crew ?

It's exciting to get on an airplane, but before you settle down to some serious fun, pay attention to the cabin crew. After they have locked (or "armed") the aircraft's doors, they give a demonstration of the safety equipment you can use on board. This includes how to put on and inflate the lifejacket under your seat and how to buckle your seatbelt. If you miss something, the information is on a card in the pocket in front of you.

A lifejacket.

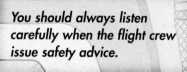

You should always listen carefully when the flight crew issue safety advice.

FACT BYTES

The Boeing 777 is the only aircraft that has never had an accident!

A jumbo jet at 37,000 feet (11,277 km) is one of the safest places to be.

How does a pilot "crash land"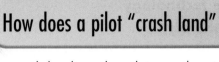

In a crash landing, the pilot uses the aircraft's wings and fuselage to absorb the shock. Passengers use their seat belts and any handy padding to protect themselves. The pilot can also use small trees and manmade structures to break the force of impact. Just before impact, the airplane should be gliding as slow and as straight as possible to avoid a sudden stop.

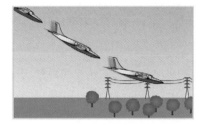

Structures break impact.

Why do aircraft crash

Over 70 percent of crashes are caused by "pilot error." This is when the pilot makes a mistake, usually during landing. Mechanical failure and bad weather also cause crashes. On March 27 1977, 583 people died in an air disaster in Tenerife. Now air controllers and pilots talk to each other in English to avoid misunderstandings.

Planes can turn into fireballs.

Who investigates plane accidents ?

Whenever there is an accident, an investigation team is formed. The team is made up of experts from the country in which the crash happened, as well as experts from the aircraft's manufacturer and airline. The team's task is to discover the cause of the accident and stop it happening again. They use the indestructible "black box" from the airplane to discover what happened.

The "black box" records all the aircraft's data for the flight.

SAFETY FIRST

HELPING HANDS

Airplanes are full of incredible technology, but the skills of the pilot and the air traffic controller are still important for a safe flight.

Why is the control tower important ❓

Staff working inside the tower guide aircraft approaching the airport using radar and computers. At take off and landing, air traffic controllers must rely on their own vision to check what's happening, and need good eyesight and quick minds. They must be able to visualize where each airplane is in relation to every other—both on runways and in the air around the airport. This is called "having the picture." After the airplane lands, someone called the ground controller directs the plane to a "gate."

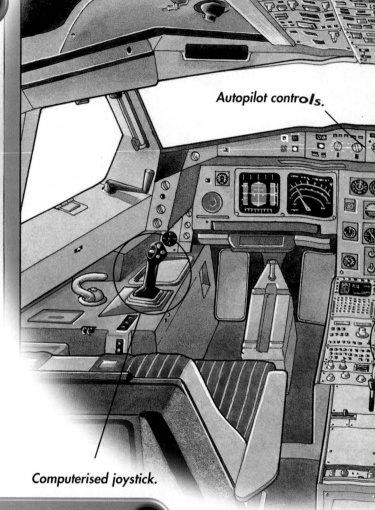

Autopilot controls.

Computerised joystick.

An air traffic controller.

How does the pilot navigate ❓

The first aviators used compasses to navigate. Gadgets called gyroscopes, which stay in one position when other things around them move, are now used in "on-board" instruments to keep aircraft on course. A gyroscope detects and corrects changes in all directions and is the basis of the inertial navigation system of an airplane. An airplane also has navigation systems based on radio waves and satellite roadcasts.

A simple gyroscope.

FACT BYTES

The word "gyroscope" comes from ancient Greek and means "circle-watcher."

GPS technology is accurate to 65.5 feet (20 m) and is also used in smart bombs.

Overhead controls.

Engine throttles.

How does "fly-by-wire" work ?

Pilots used to fly using foot pedals and a large joystick. When the pilot moved these, wires and gears in the fuselage would move aircraft parts like wings. In modern planes, computers control these movements and this is called "fly-by-wire." The pilot moves a small joystick that tells the computer what to move, and the computer uses electronic signals to move it. This allows the pilot to maneuver the plane very precisely, and is easier on the arms!

A joystick.

What is GPS ?

Global Positioning System or GPS is a satellite-based navigation system. The GPS calculates an aircraft's position using space satellite signals that tell the precise time. The aircraft then tells other aircraft and flight controllers its own position. This reduces the risk of collisions and makes aircraft less dependent on navigation from the ground.

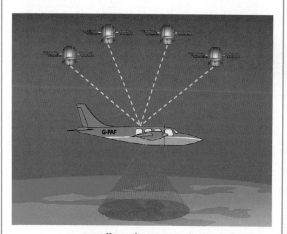

Satellites locate a plane's position.

Who is the autopilot ?

The autopilot isn't a person but a special sort of compass that can be used to keep an aircraft going in one direction at one altitude. The pilot switches to autopilot when the aircraft has reached something called "cruise altitude," which is the height at which most of the flight takes place. Then the pilot can relax and have some dinner! Modern autopilots can do nearly everything, from taking off and landing to navigating in hazardous conditions.

ATLANTIC ANTICS

The Atlantic Ocean is one of the largest and most dangerous oceans on Earth, but that hasn't stopped pilots from trying to fly between Europe and America.

Capt. Alcock and Lt. Brown.

When was the first Atlantic crossing ❓

Two British officers, Captain John Alcock and Lieutenant Arthur W. Brown, became the first people to make a non-stop flight across the Atlantic, on May 31 1919. Their airplane made the historic flight in under sixteen hours. The airplane was badly damaged when the men landed in a swamp. The officers won £10,000 and were knighted for their feat.

FACT BYTES

At times during Lindbergh's flight, the *Spirit of St Louis* was just 10 feet (3 m) above the waves of the Atlantic Ocean!

Concorde was the fastest commercial plane across the Atlantic. Concorde flew from New York to London in 2 hours 53 minutes on February 7 1996.

Charles Lindbergh in 1927.

What is the *Spirit of St Louis* ❓

The *Spirit of St. Louis* is the airplane in which Charles Lindbergh made the first solo, non-stop transatlantic flight. The flight on May 20-21 1927 took 34 hours and covered 3,610 miles (5,808 km). Lindbergh won $25,000 for this incredible adventure and became an international hero.

Charles Lindbergh's plane, the Spirit of St. Louis.

When was the fastest crossing

The supersonic spy plane SR-71 Blackbird made the fastest ever transatlantic flight in 1974. Reaching speeds of 2,193.2 mph (3,529.6 km/h), the Blackbird crossed in an amazing one hour 55 minutes!

SR-71 Blackbird.

Who was Amelia Earhart

On June 19 1928, Amelia Earhart became the first woman to cross the Atlantic. Four years later, on May 21 1932, she became the first woman to fly solo across the Atlantic. Amelia Earhart flew from Newfoundland for almost fifteen hours, before landing in Northern Ireland.

Amelia Earhart.

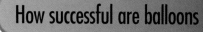
— *Alcock and Brown's transatlantic flight.*

How successful are balloons

Balloons have only recently succeeded in crossing the Atlantic. The first UK transatlantic balloon flight attempt took place in 1978 and the first solo transatlantic balloon flight took place in September 1984. There have also been several attempts to cross the Atlantic in microlights, but so far no one has succeeded.

Large, transatlantic hot-air balloons.

ATLANTIC ANTICS

31

THE NEED FOR SPEED

The quest for increasingly fast aircraft has turned the dream of space flight into reality and pilots into astronauts! Since 1947, the sound barrier has been broken and "supersonic" speeds achieved—what will be next?

When was the sound barrier broken ?

The speed of sound was reached by a plane on October 14 1947. The X-1 airplane broke the sound barrier at 45,000 feet (13,716 m). The X-1 was shaped like a bullet so that the drag would be as small as possible. The X-1 had straight, very thin wings and it was powered by a rocket engine.

The rocket-driven X-1 broke the sound barrier.

The SR-71 Blackbird is the fastest jet in the world.

What does supersonic mean ?

Sounds travel at a certain speed, 741.4 mph (1192.9 km/h). This speed is called Mach 1. A jet aircraft that travels at Mach 1 or above is called "supersonic," while an airplane that travels slower than Mach 1 is called "subsonic." There are aircraft that fly at Mach 5 (five times the speed of sound) or above. These aircraft are flown by astronauts and are called "hypersonic."

Which are the fastest aircraft ?

The SR-71 Blackbird travels at over Mach 3, and is the fastest jet in the world. The X-15 is the fastest rocket-powered aircraft. It travels at Mach 6.7. The X-15 was used to help develop space travel aircraft like the Space Shuttle. NASA's Space Shuttle travels between 18,000 mph (28,962 km/h) and Mach 10. and is designed to be a manned, reusuable launch vehicle for research and Earth-orbiting experiments.

Why has Concorde gone out of service ?

Concorde was the only supersonic airliner in the world. It traveled at twice the speed of sound and only took three and a half hours to cross the Atlantic. However, supersonic flight is very expensive because it uses so much fuel. Most people today want to travel by airplane as cheaply as possible, even when flying long distances. So Concorde was too expensive to run, despite being fantastic!

The de-commissioned Concorde.

The X-15 is the fastest rocket-powered aircraft in the world.

Why is hypersonic flight dangerous ?

Hypersonic speeds expose pilots and aircraft to incredible pressure and heat. At these speeds, pilots wear special suits and use oxygen equipment to keep them alive. Their aircraft must be made out of strong materials that reflect the heat. Supersonic aircraft need a thin body, but hypersonic aircraft like the Space Shuttle need thicker bodies.

The "sonic boom."

The Space Shuttle.

THE NEED FOR SPEED

SILENT AND DEADLY

These incredibly fast airplanes can spy on an enemy from 10 miles (16 km) up in the sky. Or they can slip through radar and destroy a target on the ground.

What is a stealth airplane

Aircraft are detected by radar, which pumps signal waves into the air. These waves bounce off an aircraft and then return to the radar tower, where the size and position of the aircraft is recorded. Stealth aircraft have many ways of escaping radar. They can also escape heat-seeking missiles.

Stealth aircraft can escape radar.

The U-2 spy plane flew too high for radar.

Radar works by bouncing radio waves off aircraft.

What are they used for ?

The Americans used a plane called the U-2 to spy on the Russians in the 1950s. They wanted to find out how many nuclear missiles the Russians had. The U-2 was a stealth plane simply because it flew too high for Russian interceptor fighters. The U-2 was recently used in both Gulf Wars to look for Iraqi missiles.

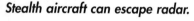

FACT BYTES

The cameras on a SR-71 Blackbird can photograph a golf ball from 80,000 feet (24,384 m)!

An F-117 stealth bomber was shot down over Yugoslavia in 1999—so stealth doesn't always work!

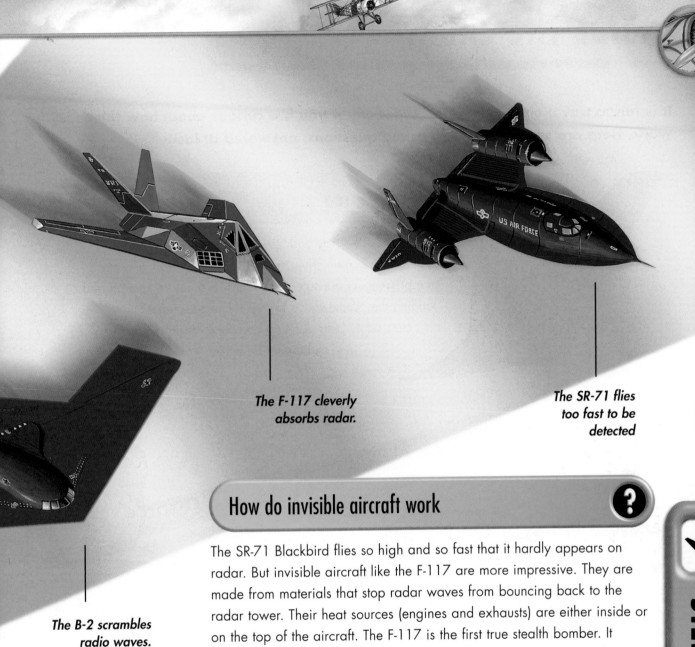

The F-117 cleverly absorbs radar.

The SR-71 flies too fast to be detected

The B-2 scrambles radio waves.

How do invisible aircraft work ❓

The SR-71 Blackbird flies so high and so fast that it hardly appears on radar. But invisible aircraft like the F-117 are more impressive. They are made from materials that stop radar waves from bouncing back to the radar tower. Their heat sources (engines and exhausts) are either inside or on the top of the aircraft. The F-117 is the first true stealth bomber. It helped win the first Gulf War.

What is a flying wing ❓

Other stealth aircraft use a "flying wing" design—the whole airplane looks like a big wing. This makes the aircraft look smaller and helps to disguise it. The most famous flying wing is the Northrop B-2 Stealth Bomber, which is probably the most sophisticated airplane ever built. The B-2 scrambles radar waves, mixing them up to confuse the radar tower.

A stealth bomber.

What about the future ❓

In the years to come, spy planes will be unmanned and travel at speeds of Mach 15. An aircraft called the X-43A is being built at the moment. This is a supersonic jet aircraft that works in space. It will run on hydrogen rather than rocket fuel. Aircraft like this will travel round the world in 90 minutes!

Future planes could run on hydrogen.

INSIDE THE CABIN

It is fun to travel on a jet airliner, especially if you are curious about how things work. Here are some frequently asked questions, answered at last!

Who are the cabin crew ?

The cabin crew are the stewards and stewardesses who look after passengers in the cabin. They serve drinks and meals and make sure passengers are safe at all times. Just before take off and landing they come round to make sure passengers have their safety belts done up correctly. Air cabin crew have to be willing to work very long hours.

Why does ice form on the windows ?

The higher the airplane flies, the colder the air outside the airplane gets. At 35,000 feet (10,668 m) the air outside can be –150°F (–65°C). It doesn't feel that cold inside the cabin because the cabin is heated, but airplanes can still be quite cold. That is why you should always have a sweater with you when flying!

Ice can form outside the airplane.

FACT BYTES

Flying supersonically heats the airplane— Concorde never has ice on cabin windows during its flight.

Why do your ears pop when flying ?

Your ears are full of air. During flight, the air inside the cabin is squashed or "pressurized." This lowers the pressure on the airplane, making it safer to fly at high altitudes. When your ears pop, you are feeling the air pressure changing in your ears. Yawning, or chewing gum will help equalize the pressure in your head.

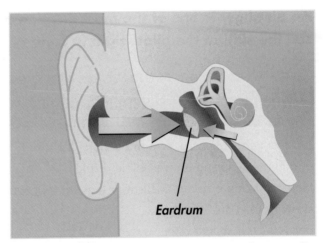

Eardrum

The pressure in your ears changes when you fly.

Who are the flight crew ?

The most senior member of the flight crew on board is the captain. He is the main pilot of the airplane. The captain introduces himself to the passengers at the beginning of the flight and is responsible for everyone on board. The captain is assisted in the cockpit by a co-pilot and a navigator. Another senior member of the flight crew is the purser.

The cabin crew serve refreshments and ensure safety.

The captain, co-pilot and navigator sit in the cockpit.

Inside the cockpit.

What is jet lag ?

When you travel around the world in a jet airliner, you can suffer from jet lag. This is when the time difference between continents or "time zones" disrupts your body clock. This can make you feel very tired. To avoid jet lag it is important to sleep on the airplane, drink lots of water and get up from your seat to stretch and walk.

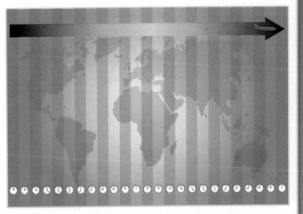

Traveling by plane can mean crossing time zones.

SHOWING OFF

An air show is one of the most exciting places you will ever visit because you can see the skill of the pilots right in front of you!

When were the first aerobatic displays ?

Just five years after the Wright brothers' flight at Kitty Hawk, stunt aviators were touring rural America and Europe, putting on incredible displays of air acrobatics (or "aerobatics"). It is because of these amazing displays of bravery that flight became popular. Many famous aviators started out in the "flying circuses" that toured after World War One.

FACT BYTES

Both Charles Lindbergh and Amelia Earhart trained in flying circuses.

Barnstormers got their name from flying through barns and hangars—open at both ends of course!

What is a barnstormer ?

Early American stunt aviators, called barnstormers, would do very dangerous stunts like jumping from a speeding car onto a ladder hanging from an airplane. Women barnstormers specialized in "wing walking"— standing on the wing of a plane while it performed a "loop," or a full circle. Both the wingwalker and the plane would turn upside down!

Modern-day barnstormers.

What is the ultimate stunt ?

Daredevil Ormer Locklear performed the "Dance of Death," which is probably the most exciting and dangerous aerial stunt ever. Locklear would fly one plane right next to another flying plane. With the wings of the aircraft almost touching and the controls locked in place, the two pilots would run along the wings, jump across to the other airplane and change places!

Ormer Locklear.

Who is Patty Wagstaff ❓

Patty Wagstaff is the most famous aerobat in the world today. Her thrilling displays have been seen by millions of air show visitors. Patty is the first woman to become America's National Aerobatic Champion, and has won gold, silver, and bronze medals in aerobatics competitions.

Patty Wagstaff.

FACT BYTES

Patty Wagstaff flies an airplane called the Extra 260 (right), which can roll over 360 degrees in a second!

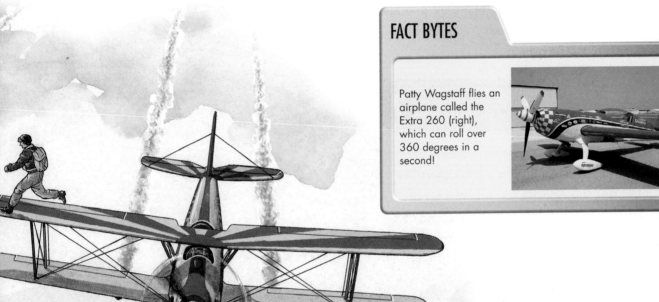

The amazing "Dance of Death."

Who are the Red Arrows ❓

The Red Arrows are the Royal Air Force's Aerobatic Team, the most famous aerial display team. During their show, the Red Arrows fly nine Hawk T1 aircraft in a diamond formation. Other maneuvers include the Synchro—in which two Hawks cross in front of the crowd— and the Vixen Loop. The Red Arrows have flown 3,500 shows in 50 countries.

The Diamond.

The Synchro.

The Vixen Loop.

HELICOPTERS

Helicopters can do much more than airplanes, but they are a lot slower and very difficult to fly.

The Cobra has rocket launchers, missiles, and cannon.

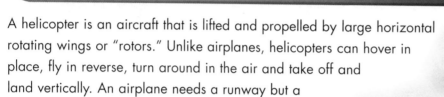

What is a helicopter ?

A helicopter is an aircraft that is lifted and propelled by large horizontal rotating wings or "rotors." Unlike airplanes, helicopters can hover in place, fly in reverse, turn around in the air and take off and land vertically. An airplane needs a runway but a helicopter can land anywhere.

What are helicopters used for ?

Helicopters were used to transport soldiers during the Vietnam War. Today, military helicopters like the Cobra and the Apache can fire missiles at enemy targets. Civilian helicopters fight fires and rescue people lost in mountains or at sea. Helicopters can carry heavy loads in a basket beneath their bodies. The police use helicopters to chase criminals and film crews use them for filming from the air.

Helicopters are useful for fighting fires.

Helicopters are essential in many rescue operations.

The Apache is a two-person attack helicopter.

FACT BYTES

The rotors of French and Russian helicopters turn counter-clockwise, while those on British and American helicopters turn clockwise.

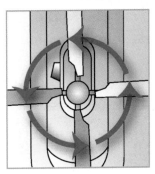

A rotor turning counter-clockwise.

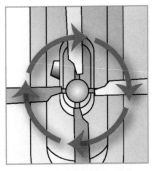

A rotor turning clockwise.

How are they controlled ?

Helicopters lift off the ground with the help of rotors, which can be angled to send the helicopter in different directions. The pilot has flight controls called the "collective" and the "cyclic." The collective controls the angle of the rotors together and makes the helicopter go up and down. The cyclic controls the angle of the rotors separately and makes the helicopter go forward, backward, left, and right.

Cyclic control stick

Collective controls

Rotors lift the helicopter off the ground.

How does a helicoptor hover ?

Hovering in a helicopter requires experience and skill. The pilot adjusts the cyclic to maintain the helicopter's position and adjusts the collective to maintain altitude. The pilot adjusts foot pedals that control a tail rotor. The tail rotor allows the helicopter to rotate but during a hover, it maintains the direction in which the helicopter is pointing.

Will helicoptors replace planes ?

It is unlikely that helicopters will ever replace airplanes: they aren't very fast because of the immense drag produced by their rotors. They are also noisy and vibrate a lot. In fact, a helicopter can shake itself to pieces! Compared to other aircraft, helicopters are difficult to fly and more expensive to buy. Future helicopters may have jets as well as rotors to make them faster and quieter.

FACT BYTES

The MH-53J "Pave Low" helicopter is the most technologically advanced model in the world, and is an updated version of the "Super Jolly Green Giant" used in the Vietnam War.

31264

HELICOPTERS

OTHER WAYS TO FLY

Imagine soaring like an eagle thousands of feet above the ground. Although the air is a bit chilly, the view is fantastic!

Hang gliders are lifted by "thermals."

The pilot steers the hang glider by moving their body.

How do hang gliders work ❓

A hang glider is a triangular wing with a frame. The hang glider has no engine, so the pilot must run down a slope to take off. Once airborne, hang gliders get lift from thermals. The pilot is suspended from the hang glider by a harness, and maneuvers by shifting his or her weight in the required direction.

FACT BYTES

The designer of the hang glider was inspired by a waterskier who used a kite to lift himself out of the water.

In order to stop, the pilot has to tip their body backwards.

How far can they fly ❓

Using thermals, a pilot may stay in the air for many hours and fly as high as 16,000 feet (4,876 m). If pilots fly above 10,000 feet (3,048 m), they will need oxygen equipment. On June 20, 2002, Mike Barber flew his hang-glider 437 miles (703 km), which is the longest flight ever made by hang glider.

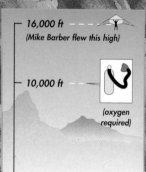

16,000 ft
(Mike Barber flew this high)

10,000 ft

(oxygen required)

What is the easiest way to fly ?

A paraglider has no frame—it is just a wing and a harness and looks like a parachute. Paragliding is the easiest way to fly: the basic techniques of launching, turning, and landing are very easy to learn. Paragliding is popular because it is affordable and you can pack your very own aircraft into a large bag!

What are microlights ?

If you put a motor on a hang glider you have a microlight. A microlight is likely to have a small fuselage with a cockpit and an engine under the wing. This is sometimes called a trike unit. The microlight may be the answer to the dream of flying—a low cost machine that everyone can fly!

A low-cost microlight.

A paraglider looks like a parachute.

Who invented unpowered flight ?

In the 1960s, an American engineer called Francis Melvin Rogallo was working on ways to recover space rockets after finishing their missions in space. He designed the wing that is used today in hang gliders and most other forms of "unpowered" flight (which means "flight without engines"). This wing shape is called the delta flexwing.

Melvin Rogallo with the delta flexwing.

FACT BYTES

In 1976, American John Moody designed an ultralight kit which set the standard for many microlights. He is known as the "father of ultralights" and has a flying award named after him.

OTHER WAYS TO FLY

THE FUTURE OF FLIGHT

It was only one hundred years ago that man turned the dream of flight into reality. How many of today's dreams will become tomorrow's realities?

What are space planes

Since 1998, researchers have been designing a hypersonic space airplane called Hypersoar. Hypersoar will travel in Earth's atmosphere to carry passengers, spy or drop bombs. It will travel at 6,700 mph (10,780 km/h), or Mach 10, and fly at between 115,000-200,000 feet (35,000-60,000 m). The bomber version would be able to carry almost 100,000 lb (45,000 kg) of bombs. Hypersoar may even be nuclear powered!

The shape of things to come?

What comes after stealth

"Morphing" or shape-changing aircraft will be made out of materials called "shape memory alloys." These alloys can change shape and then return to their original form. So, a spy plane could change into a fighter-bomber in mid flight! Another stealth advancement is in quiet supersonic flight. Soon, supersonic aircraft will have nose globes that will stop the noise of sonic boom.

Shape-changing aircraft are possibly the next step.

"Hypersoar" could carry passengers into space.

How will the pilot's job change

In the future, the pilot's helmet will provide all the information the pilot needs to fly. A map of the sky will be painted onto the pilot's retina using lazers. This will give the pilot complete awareness of his or her surroundings. Instead of just seeing information, pilots will feel it, because they will be wearing suits that vibrate when certain things happen.

A futuristic helmet?

Why are the Wright brothers back in fashion ?

On December 17 2003, it was 100 years since the Wright brothers flew their first airplane. Now, for the first time, their ideas about wing warping are being used in modern aircraft. "Active aeroelastic wings" are wings that are made out of very light but strong materials. They can be twisted to control the aircraft, as the Wright brothers proved at Kitty Hawk!

The Wright brothers.

What about air safety ?

Computer technologies are being developed to make flying much safer. One of these shows the pilot the situation on the ground and in the air in clear daylight, even in the worst weather conditions. Airplane manufacturers are working on a system that will predict the failure of aircraft parts, allowing them to be replaced before they fail.

Flight technology is constantly being developed.

FACT BYTES

The Pelican, the world's largest cargo airplane, will be able to carry seventeen tanks!

Unmanned combat air vehicles will replace the RAF's Tornado fleet by 2020.

THE FUTURE OF FLIGHT

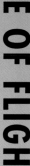

GLOSSARY

Air Traffic Control
System to mark where planes are in the sky.

Autopilot
A piece of equipment that keeps the plane cruising at a consistent height.

Aviator
A pilot who flies an aircraft: an airman or an airwoman.

Barnstormers
The name given to early US stunt aviators.

Battle of Britain
It took place in 1940 during the Second World War between the forces of Germany and Great Britain.

Black Box
A piece of electronic equipment which records all the flight details of an aircraft and is important when a crash is investigated.

Circumnavigate
To sail, or fly, completely around.

Cruise Altitude
This is the height at which a plane travels for the longest part of its journey.

Dance of Death
An exciting aerial stunt performed by two pilots in planes flying very closely alongside each other. Each pilot locks the controls in place, then runs along the wings and changes places to pilot the other one's aircraft.

Drag
The frictional force of air moving past the aircraft, which slows it down.

Fuselage
The main body of an aircraft carrying the crew and the passengers.

GPS
The Global Positioning System is a satellite-based navigation system that is used to calculate the precise position of an aircraft.

Gyroscope
A small flywheel that resists any change in motion.

Hawker Harrier
The first operational vertical/short take off and landing military aircraft.

Hindenburg
A hydrogen-filled airship built by the German government in 1936. It carried 72 passengers and made 63 successful flights most of them across the Atlantic Ocean; but caught fire in 1937.

Hypersonic
Describes an aircraft or rocket capable of flying at a speed faster than Mach 5.

Interceptor
A small, light aircraft that is used to intercept approaching enemy aircraft.

Joystick
The control lever used in the piloting of an aircraft.

Kamikaze
The name given to a Japanese plane, or pilot, loaded with explosives that deliberately crashes into an enemy target. Originated from the Second World War.

Lift
An upward force created by the movement of the air around an aircraft's wings.

Mach
Usually followed by a number to express the ratio of aircraft's speed to the speed of sound.

Microlight
A lightweight, small engined aircraft, rather like a powered hang glider.

Morphing
Transforming one shape into another. In planes this means using shape memory alloys which change then return to their original shape.

Ornithopter
The Italian artist Leonardo da Vinci designed this flying machine.

Paragliding
The sport of gliding using a parachute with specially-shaped wings.

Radar
The use of radio waves for navigation purposes.

Red Arrows
A British aerobatics team formed in 1964 with seven display pilots. In 1968 two more pilots joined and became famous for flying in a "Diamond Nine" formation.

Red Baron
The name given to Manfred von Richthofen, a German pilot who flew his bright-red painted aircraft during World War One.

Rotors
The blades projecting from a cylinder which rotate at high speed to provide the force to lift and propel a helicopter.

Smart Bombs
A smart weapon is equipped with hi-tech systems designed to direct it with precision to its target.

Sonic Boom
The loud boom heard when a plane passes through the sound barrier.

Spirit of St Louis
The first plane to fly non-stop across the Atlantic, from New York to Paris on May 20 1927.

Stealth Aircraft
They can avoid detection radar; even escaping the specialist "heat-seeking" missiles.

Stratosphere
The layer of Earth's atmosphere that extends from about 7 miles to about 31 miles above Earth's surface and contains the ozone layer.

Subsonic
Flying at less than the speed of sound.

Supersonic
Traveling faster than the speed of sound.

Thermals
A rising current of warm air used by gliders and hang gliders to move upwards.

Thrust
The forward force created by the aircraft's engines, which move it forwards.

Time Zones
The 24 parallel longitudinal sections into which the world is divided. All places within a given zone generally have the same standard time.

Transatlantic
To cross from one side of the Atlantic ocean to another.

Vertical Take off
A fixed-wing aircraft specially designed for taking off directly upwards from a stationary position, often the deck of a ship.

Wing walking
Performed by the barnstomers—particularly women. They stood on the aircraft's wings while it did a "loop" (turned upside down).

Zeppelin
A cigar shaped, hydrogen-filled airship designed by Ferdinand von Zeppelin.

GLOSSARY

INDEX

Key: Top - t; middle - m; bottom - b; left - l; right -r.
Front Cover: Gary Slaters/SpecArt. Back cover: (tl, ml, mr, bl) Gary Slaters/SpecArt; (tr) Meme Design; (br) Aviation Picture Library.
1: Meme Design. 2: (m) NASA; (ml, b) Meme Design. 3 - 6: Meme Design. 7: (t, ml) Meme Design; (mr) NASA. 8: Meme Design. 9: (t, bl) Meme Design; (m) Sunil Gupta; (br) NASA. 10: Meme Design. 11: (t, br) Airbus; (bl) Meme Design. 12 - 13: Meme Design. 14: Meme Design. 15: (t) Airbus; (b) Meme Design. 16 - 17: Meme Design. 18: (t) Meme Design; (b) Aviation Picture Library. 19: (bl) Corel; (t, b) Meme Design. 20: Meme Design. 21: (t, m) Meme Design; (br) Meme Design, NASA and Steve Williams. 22 - 27: Meme Design. 28: (m) Meme Design; (b) Photodisc. 29: (tr) Airbus; (tl, br) Meme Design. 30: Meme Design. 31: (t) Courtesy of Lockheed Martin; (m) Meme Design; (b) Courtesy of Cameron Balloons. 32: Meme Design. 33: (t) Courtesy of Joe Napoli; (bl) Meme Design; (br) NASA. 34: Meme Design. 35: (t, br) Meme Design; (bl) Courtesy of Northrop Grumman. 36: (m, bl) Meme Design; (br) Sunil Gupta. 37: (t, b) Meme Design; (m) Topham Picturepoint. 38: (t, br) Meme Design; (bl) Courtesy of Brian Condon. 39: (t, mr) Courtesy of Patty Wagstaff; (ml, b) Meme Design. 40: Meme Design. 41: (t, m) Meme Design; (br) DigitalVision. 42: Meme Design. 43: (t) Meme Design; (b) NASA. 44: Meme Design. 45: (t) NASA; (m) Airbus; (b) Meme Design. 46 - 48: Meme Design.

Inside illustrations by Mike Thomas/ Meme Design.